Ransom Neutron Stars
New Kinds of Energy
by Jill Atkins

Published by Ransom Publishing Ltd.
Unit 7, Brocklands Farm, West Meon, Hampshire GU32 1JN, UK
www.ransom.co.uk

ISBN   978 178591 434 8
First published in 2017
Reprinted 2018

There is a reading comprehension quiz available for this book in the popular
Accelerated Reader® software system. For information about ATOS, Accelerated
Reader, quiz points and reading levels please visit www.renaissance.com. Accelerated
Reader, AR, the Accelerated Reader Logo, and ATOS are trademarks of Renaissance
Learning, Inc. and its subsidiaries, registered common law or applied for in the U.S.
and other countries. Used under license.

New Kinds
of Energy

Jill Atkins

We need coal, gas and oil to get energy for our cars and homes, and to keep us warm.

Coal, gas and oil come from the fossils of organisms that died millions of years ago. Now they lie deep under the ground or under the sea. People must dig or drill them out.

Coal

You can burn coal to heat your house, to cook or to heat water.

Coal is found in seams under the ground. It looks like black stone.

Men go deep down into a coal mine to dig the coal out. They travel down in a cage, with hard hats, torches and tools. It is hard work.

Gas and oil

Gas and oil have to be drilled out of the ground.

If the gas or oil is under the sea (such as the North Sea), people erect a platform or rig.

They travel from the land by helicopter or boat to reach the platform. Then they live and work on the rig.

An oil rig

The workers drill into the oil under the
sea and the rig sucks the oil or gas out.
The oil or gas is fed into container ships
or tankers.

Sometimes, it will go along a pipeline
to reach land.

Some workers must dive deep down under the water to check on the drill and pipes. This is a very risky job.

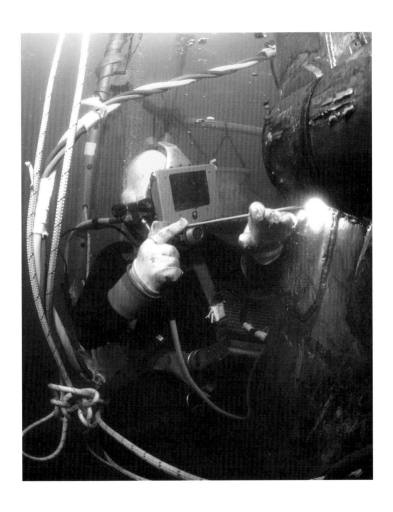

Gas comes along pipes into places such as shops, hospitals and homes for heating and cooking.

Oil is made into petrol for cars, trucks, buses and ships. Oil can power electric things, like toasters, lights, computers and cookers, too.

It is also made into plastic toys, bags, boxes and many different plastic things.

People are drilling everywhere as they try to find oil and gas. It is a very hot topic!

Different leaders want all the oil they can find. This might mean drilling in the Arctic.

This would be a big problem for the wildlife in the Arctic, as the sea ice might melt and the water might no longer be clean. The oil might get everywhere!

Coal, oil and gas can pollute land, sea and air in many ways.

✳ Oil can pollute the ground around it.

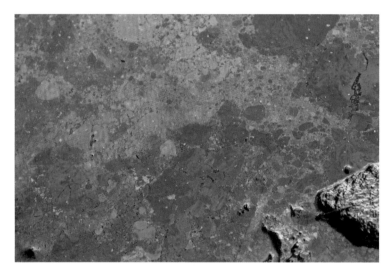

✳ An oil spill at sea will pollute the water and a lot of wildlife might die.

✷ Plastic can kill wildlife if they eat it
or get trapped in it.

✷ Coal smoke can make smog (a
mix of fog and smoke). This is bad
for the lungs.

Smog

Apart from all that, there is a different problem, and it is a big problem.

Coal, oil and gas will run out in the end. It will all get used up.

But when? How much is left in the ground? We just don't know.

What will people do for power when there is no gas, oil or coal? How will we cope?

People are trying to find new kinds of energy.

When people split the atom, a new kind of power was born – atomic power.

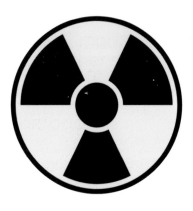

This power can be made into very strong energy, so-called 'clean energy'.

But this kind of energy can have its problems, too.

An atomic power plant

If there were a meltdown, like there was in Japan a few years ago, it would poison the air and contaminate the land around it for millions of years.

There would be "fall out" from the meltdown.

Many people might become very ill or die.

So can we find different ways to make power?

✳ Wind farms are constructed to harness the power of the wind. The wind never runs out!

But some people say the turbines are ugly and spoil their outlook.

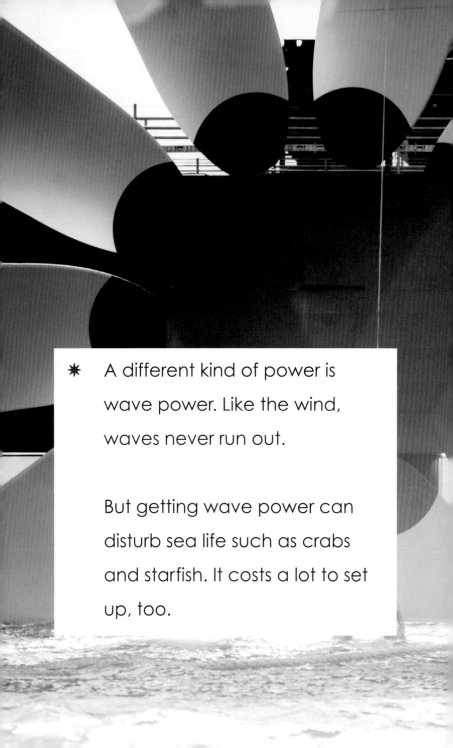

✻ A different kind of power is wave power. Like the wind, waves never run out.

But getting wave power can disturb sea life such as crabs and starfish. It costs a lot to set up, too.

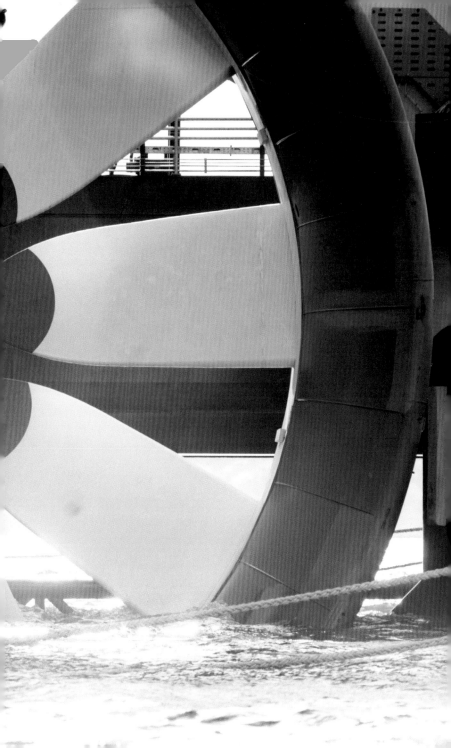

THIS SALE

£ 00000

00000

00000

✳ Rape seed oil and linseed oil can be made into a different kind of plastic.

These oils might be a good fuel for cars, too.

Will a new power be found soon? People need to find a new kind of energy quickly, because gas, coal and oil cannot last for ever!

Have you read?

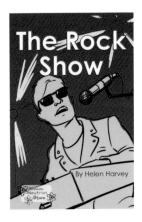

The Rock Show

by Helen Harvey

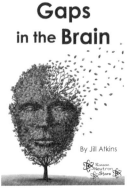

Gaps in the Brain

by Jill Atkins

Have you read?

G B H

by Jill Atkins

Steel Pan Traffic Jam

by Cath Jones

Ransom Neutron Stars

New Kinds of Energy
Word count **688**

Covers:
Letters and Sounds Phase 5

Phonics

Phonics 1	Not Pop, Not Rock Go to the Laptop Man Gus and the Tin of Ham	*Phonics 2*	Deep in the Dark Woods Night Combat Ben's Jerk Chicken Van
Phonics 3	GBH Steel Pan Traffic Jam Platform 7	*Phonics 4*	The Rock Show Gaps in the Brain **New Kinds of Energy**

Book bands

Pink	Curry! Free Runners My Toys	*Red*	Shopping with Zombies Into the Scanner Planting My Garden
Yellow	Fit for Love The Lottery Ticket In the Stars	*Blue*	Awesome ATAs Wolves The Giant Jigsaw
Green	Fly, May FLY! How to Start Your Own Crazy Cult The Care Home	*Orange*	Text Me The Last Soldier Best Friends